4 MONTHS AND 10 DAYS

by Na'ima B. Robert

SISTERS
AWAKENING
PRESS

4 MONTHS AND 10 DAYS
Published by Sisters Awakening Press

Sisters Awakening Press
Gautam House
1-3 Shenley Avenue
Ruislip
HA4 6BP
UK

A CIP catalogue record for this book is available from the British Library.
ISBN 978-0-9933195-2-5

Dedication

A thousand tears have I shed
For the one
For whom
I sang a thousand songs.

Contents

Introduction

There is a delicate tension in the state of iddah, the mourning period for a widow.

On the one hand, life continues, particularly if you have children or have to work to support your family. The pressures, demands, and responsibilities are real and they won't wait for four months and ten days to be over. In this space, you are forced to plan, look forward, move on, and face the world. It can be an exquisite distraction from the pain that's buried deep beneath the school run, bedtime stories, and endless paperwork and deadlines.

But it is still a distraction.

On the other hand, your state of iddah restricts you; you cannot fully embrace life, even if you wanted to. You must pause. You

must reflect.
You must withdraw.

You must face the reality and brave the darkness: the ache, the loneliness, the anger, the fear, the feeling of being bereft. You must face it because it will break you down, bring you to your knees, make you feel once again that vulnerability of his last days when you would have given anything for one last apology, one last kiss, one last promise. You must face the reality that this is Allah's plan for you. And that, if this is so, there must be khair in it for you. It's there. It's there in the chance to ask for forgiveness, to pour your heart out, to cleanse, to rectify your soul, to purify your habits, to be ready to emerge from your iddah like a butterfly from a chrysalis: reborn, refashioned, beautiful.
For it is only through being tested that we realise our true selves.

I pray this book serves as a reminder to the reader of the brevity of this life, of the need to treat every day, every moment as precious and, most importantly, to love with all your heart for the sake of Allah. Those that you love are not promised to you for a lifetime; they are gifts that belong to Allah ta'ala. He lends them to us for an appointed time. Cherish them with every fibre of your being.

Your sister in Islam, in life and love,
Na'ima B. Robert

November 2016

Before...

Betrayal

I can sleep at night.
I can eat and drink.
I can laugh with my sister until my sides ache.
I can forget.
But then I remember.
Then I feel like a traitor.
And then I cry like a baby.

One More Chance

Today
I dared
To ask
For one more chance.
One more chance
To say 'Yes'
Instead of 'No';
One more chance to say 'I'm listening'
Instead of 'I know';
One more chance to hold on
Instead of letting go.
Will I get another chance?
I don't know.
Did I waste my last chance?
I don't know.
Is this your last chance?
You don't know.
You just
Don't
Know.

Two Weeks In

The words are like water:
At times
They flow effortlessly
Slipping over stones in a stream.
At other times
They trickle,
Painstaking,
Drop by drop by drop
Until the flow resumes,
Because then
The words are a waterfall
Gushing forth
A wall of wonder
At one with the world
At one with the Word
At one with the tears

That gush forth
Like waterfalls
To wash away my worries
To wean me off the pain
To purify
To clarify
To cleanse me once again.
Word after blessed word
Until minutes turn to hours
And my hand is damp in yours.
Baqarah for protection,
Kahf because it's Friday
And it's been two weeks
And I miss you.

Iddah...

A part of me died last week.
But, alhamdulillah, it wasn't hope. It wasn't courage. And it definitely wasn't faith and trust in my Lord's perfect plan.

Still Blessed

I feel so incredibly blessed. Even in the midst of the trial, as the tears fall, I am surrounded by His Mercy. The du'as, the support, the love, the sense of strength and serenity, are all signs of His Mercy. Alhamdulillah, I accept. Alhamdulillah, I am at peace. Alhamdulillah, alhamdulillah, alhamdulillah is the balm for my aching heart.

In Public Institutions

I must stop this
Annoying habit
Of crying
In public institutions.
This week
Alone
I have
Burst into tears
In no fewer than three
Administrative offices.
Four, if you count
British soil.
There is a desperate,
Terrifying quality
To these tears.

They are intensely private
Yet painfully public.
I gasp for air
Trying to stem
The rising tide
That threatens to drown me.
But the air is never enough:
It is dry and thin
In those offices
Of birth and marriage and death
And appointments and queues
And passports and certificates:
Birth, marriage and death.
Always the death certificate
The reason I am standing
Sitting
Waiting
In a crowded public office
Struggling to catch my breath.

The Nights

After a day
Of living in the moment
And looking to the future
And moving forward,
The night brings the past
And the pain
Seeping in,
Creeping in.
The nights are the worst.
And no matter how
You try to fill them
With the here
And now,
The past comes seeping in,
Creeping in.

Silence is Golden

I want to stop writing
I want to stop the public load shedding
But I fear that
If I stop
My teeth will grind themselves
To dust.

Drown

Go ahead,
Sink
Embrace the abyss
Allow the grief
To weigh you down
To pull at the life inside you
Until you reach the bottom
Rock bottom
Sink.
Do not think.
Do not feel.
What more is there?
What's the worst that could happen?
You could drown.
You could allow the grief

To flood your lungs
Until you cannot breathe
Until you are blind to beauty
Until you are numb to kindness
Until you are deaf to hope
And you let the water weeds
Curl tight around your legs
And keep you prisoner
At the bottom of the river.
You could drown.
Is that what you want?

Catch Me

Sweet stoicism
Stifles the screams,
Silences the sighs,
Sinks the soul
To numbness.
My heart is too hard to hurt.
My hands, too full to face the sky.
My eyes, too focused to tear up
With wild, wilful tears.
Forgive me, Lord.
Forgive me
And catch me
When my back finally breaks
When my heart finally cracks
When the tears finally fall

And fall
And fall,
Drowning me
And all my patience,
Strength
And fortitude.
When the agony of loss
Threatens to throw me from the cliff,
Catch me, Lord.
Catch me.

All Changed

It is the pain
In the voices of others
That breaks me
Because they see
What I refuse to see
What I turn away from
What my heart refuses to accept:
That my life is changed,
Changed utterly.
My other half ripped away,
My heart scoured,
Beating abrasions,
The axis of my world
Tilted
Unalterably,

The path of my journey
Detoured
Permanently.
All changed,
Changed utterly.
This is what I hear
In the voice of others,
In their pain,
In their tears,
In their silence.
They are grieving for me
Because of what they see
For how this calamity
Affects their reality.
It is my pain reflected
In the eyes of others
That breaks me.

That's why it is easier,
For now,
To turn away
And remain dry eyed
And stone hearted.
I will not be broken.
I will not.
I will not.
I…

Waves of Grief

Truly mourning him
Is a story I refuse to tell myself.
My refusal is a wall against the wave of grief
That threatens to engulf everything,
Leaving nothing but a broken hull on the shore.

How to Be a Widow

I don't know
How to be a widow.
They say widows are fragile,
Brittle as frozen regrets
Bitter as broken promises
The legacy of a life unlived.
They say widows are broken,
Needy,
Worthy of pity
And a life behind closed shutters.
They say widows are remnants,
Bleak reminders
Of the dearly departed.
Widows weaken.
Widows wane.
Widows are a constant,
aching reminder
Of the omnipresence of pain.

Well then,
If all that they say is true,
Then I thank Allah
I don't know
How to be a widow.
Alhamdulillah.

Mourn Like a Man

I want to mourn like a man
I want to be quick about it
No time to lose
Life is waiting
And the past is dead
And gone
Gone like he is.
QadrAllah.

I want to mourn like a man
Just three days
To cry, rage, despair
And cry again
And then pull myself together
Accept what is past
Past like he is.
QadrAllah.

I want to mourn like a man
No-one asking
Again and again
'How are things?'
I want people to assume
That I'm coping
Because that's what men do.
That's what he did.
QadrAllah.

I want to mourn like a man
For my heart to be unfettered
My desires justified
Understandable
No need for explanations
Or deprivations
Free to love without guilt
Like he did.
QadrAllah.

But
I am not a man
And I cannot mourn
As men are expected to.
I cannot forget
My soul companion
After three days
I cannot move on
From a lifetime of memories
After three days,
And I ask myself
Does any husband
Who has truly loved
Ever mourn like a man?

To Those on Their Own

What if you could cut out that part of you that made you woman: would
you?
Cut out that part of you that is alive
And tender
And wanting to be loved
And held and cherished: would you?
To pass between day and night
As silent and seamless as a ghost,
Cold to warm eyes
And ready smiles
And whispered promises
And secret desires: would you?
To stand straight
And tall

While others fall
to their knees,
While they surrender
To the loneliness
To the cravings,
To their needs: would you?
To never seek
Neither tongue
Nor eye,
To be aloof to the world
As it rushes by,
To never feel the pull of the heartstrings
To be far above such worldly things: would you?
And, if you did, what would that make you?

A Lone Parent

I thought I knew
How to be a lone parent.
Weeks of solitude
And business trips
And full time mothering
Have toughened my skin
And made my back strong.
But I find my back bending,
Bending almost to breaking
With this new burden:
An only parent.
A lone parent.
A lonely parent.
It is as if my compass
Is broken

I am left
Spinning wildly
Not sure which way
Is up
Or down.
When to say no,
When to say yes.
I have no-one to ask,
No-one to rant to,
No-one down here in the trenches
In heart and spirit,
If not in body.
A lonely parent
Who has lost her way,
And every day finds herself
Spinning
Spinning.

Ya Allah
Point my compass again.
By my North Star,
My guide,
My solace
In this solitude.
For, without You
I am lost
And alone.

Soldiers

For those times
When you know
That the most noble retreat
from the frontlines of your life
Is a natural death.
But since your natural demise
is not in your hands
You soldier on,
Try to stay strong,
Try to hold on,
Though your armour weighs you down
And at times
You wish you could sink with it
Into the earth
To join the bones
Of all the fallen heroes
Whose glory began
As their struggle ended.

Tell Me I Can Do This

Someone tell me I can do this.
Someone tell me that I have it in me,
That others have done more with less,
That the prize is worth the stress.
Someone tell me that God is on my side,
That He wouldn't test me with it
If I couldn't handle it.
Someone tell me that this strength is real
Not a mask,
That this confidence is divinely inspired
Not hubris,
That this is all part of a divine plan
To bring out the best in me,
To cleanse me
To purify me,

Smoothing my roughened edges
Until the jewel emerges
Shining brighter than ever before.
Someone tell me that I can do this.
Then tell me again
And, maybe then, I will believe it.

Patience

When your eyes are swollen with secret tears
And you dare not think about what tomorrow will bring
When you put on a smile
That makes you die inside,
Remember this:
There may come a time
When positivity and strength
Must give way
To pure,
Unadulterated
Patience.

Anguish

The anguish is there
In the blackness behind your eyelids
When they're squeezed tight shut
Holding back tears
Because it's too much
To take in
To accept
To believe
And you fear you may explode
If you don't take a breath
And call His name.

Alone

So you unpacked the shopping alone,
No-one to tell you to go inside and relax,
No-one to take the strain of those heavy paper bags from you,
No-one to make you a cup of tea
Once everything was packed away.
Alhamdulillah
You have shopping to carry
And put away
And turn into works of art on a plate.
So you got the plumbing fixed on your own,
No-one to complain about it to,
No-one to heap with silent accusations,
No-one to make you believe that it never was.
Alhamdulillah
You have what it takes
To wrestle
With plumbing,
And wiring,

And hiring
And firing,
Banking,
Bills,
And all the other mundane details of a responsible life.
So you tucked the children into bed alone,
No-one to read them a story,
While you supervise tooth-brushing,
No-one to give you a hug when you're done
And massage your feet
While you savour your tea.
Alhamdulillah
Those children are asleep now
And you can breathe
And be at peace,
Knowing that they know that they are loved.
So you watched the sun rise alone,
Lips moving,
Fingertips on fingertips

You marvelled at the colours
The dawn's brightness
Dimmed only by the fact
That there was no-one to share it with.
Alhamdulillah
You have a soul that soars at the sight of the sunrise.
Alhamdulillah for the sunrise.
Alhamdulillah for your sight.
Alhamdulillah for your soul,
For your life,
For another day in it's heady embrace.
Alhamdulillah.

Shards

Going through his things
Is like
Sorting through his dreams
Which is like
Reclaiming the pain
And that's like
Going through it all again
Which is like
Sifting through shards
Of diamond-splintered glass.
You will bleed.
Of course
You will.

Dust

Dust
Has gathered
On the shoulders of your jackets.
Has it been that long?
I wipe it off
As I wipe the tears
As I fold and pack.
So many memories
Come flooding back.
The tears fall
And the shell cracks
The pressure is released and,
At last,
The voice is heard.
The voice I feared for so long:

The voice of pain,
Of anguish,
Of loneliness,
Of grief.
The grief that, for so long,
Dared not speak its name.
Now I fold your clothes
And pack away too many
(Maybe your sons will wear them
one day)
And can only bear to part
With a pitiful few.
But the reality is this:
You have left these thobes,
And these jackets,
And these cufflinks,
And they are nothing to you now.

Not even your scent clings to them.
Better to fold and pack
I can't get those days back
Just the memories remain
To bring a smile to my face
And take me back to you again.
I write poetry that you will never read
Why not pack away clothes you will never need?
Insha Allah, your sons will wear them one day,
Perhaps to the Friday prayer,
Or to their graduation,
Or to meet a nice girl's family,
Or on their wedding day.
Maybe I'll be there to iron it:
Who's to say?

For now,
We're taking it day by day,
Take nothing for granted
Better to walk this way.
Another milestone reached
On this journey of grief,
Another step forward
Towards healing and relief.
Insha Allah.

Death and Rebirth

Every new fight
That you face alone
Is like
An abrasion on the skin of your innocence.
Every bump
Against the harsh realities of life
Leaves a bruise,
Leaves your heart
Calloused
Like the palms of a hand carrying the ways of the world
In an overweight suitcase.
But you know
It must be so
For you to grow.

For new life to spring forth
Blood must be spilled
And muscles and tendons stretched
Beyond any known capacity.
Beyond imagining.
When we spill forth
We scream
Enough to tear down the skies
But who hears the silent cries of the seed
As its skin tears
To release the thirsty, insistent root
That forces its way
Deeper and deeper into the soil
Spreading
Searching
For what will give it life?

Who hears the silent cry
Of the tightly wrapped bud
As it splits open and spills
The blossoms
The petals
The perfume
That crown the morning
Of an early spring?
Who hears, indeed?
Perhaps only the One
Who created
The splitting
The spilling
The screams and the silence
The death and the rebirth
The remaking and the heart breaking
In every waking, every shaking, every taking

Everything that brought you here
Ready to step into your destiny,
Hesitant at first,
Heart sore,
Limping,
Until you realise you can bear it
Until your wings start unfolding:
Until weight becomes lightness
Until light conquers darkness
Until you see the mercy in the harshness
And the smile returns
The promised ease soothes the burns
And you're ready
To exhale.

Once Were Warriors

It's because we once were warriors,
Standing side by side,
Swords swinging left and right,
Felling foes to either side,
Back to back
You had mine,
I had yours...
It's because we once were warriors
That I feel deserted,
Abandoned,
Left alone to fight off
The hungry hordes.
And yet,
After a quiet moment of despair,
A new strength swells within me,

A strength that does not have you
As its source,
A strength that rides on
With irresistible force,
A strength that will see this trial
Run its course
Run until the enemies retreat
Run until I see the world at our feet
Run until the tears run dry
When, spent but victorious,
I give thanks and rise.
Insha Allah.

Do You Remember?

Do you remember when
We made plans?
Plans to make 'Umrah every year,
To trek across Mongolia on a motorbike,
To retire to a farm with Wi-Fi and horses,
To live on three continents,
To one day make Hajj with our children
And their spouses
And their children.
Do you remember?
Do you remember when
We put off plans?
Plans for date nights
And eating more vegetables
For fearless vulnerability

For deeper connection.
Do you remember?
I remember now
And the tears fall,
Unbidden.
Allah plans
And His plans are not like our plans.
I trust in the wisdom of His plan.
I do.
So why,
Why do I share our private plans with the world?
Because we weren't the only ones
To think that the future was ours
To plan.

Grateful for the Sweetness

It is as if
Every joyful greeting
Is the foreshadowing
Of a tearful goodbye.
It is as if
Every laughter-filled gathering
Is a reminder
Of the private tears you cry.
It is as if
I would rather
You had never come
Than to have to face
The pain of parting.
Almost.
But not quite.

Because, through the tears,
I breathe gratitude:
It quiets the quaking
And pacifies the pain.
I am grateful for the sweetness
Though it comes at the price of loss,
I will live for the moments of wonder
And I will not count the cost.
Because in the end
Our hearts will be turned to dust
Whether we loved or lost,
In the end
There will be no going over
When separated by Death's hard frost.

Celebrate Life

When every victory,
Every first time,
Every 'we made it'
Is tinged with melancholy
Because the one you lost wasn't there
To cheer with you,
To celebrate with you,
To praise with you,
Savour the victory,
Taste the triumph.
Care not for the bitter taste of loss
That threatens to curdle the sweetness of success.
It will only spoil
If you let it.

Refuse to let it.
Refuse to become jaded
After his presence has faded.
Be alive to taste
To feel
To celebrate
Life.

⊰⊱

Aluta Continua

Only by His Grace,
Only by His Mercy,
Only by the prayers
Of loved ones,
Only by the strength that is sewn
Into our sinews,
Are we still standing,
Nay, walking forward.
Aluta continua.

Older and Alone

I asked her, 'What is it like to be older and alone?' She answered, 'You must first be comfortable in your own company. You must make peace with being alone.'

'Eid Night

When she speaks of him
Her eyes light up
Still,
Her voice grows soft
Still,
The memories come rushing back
Still.
When she speaks of him,
The weight lifts:
There is joy in the lightness,
There is healing in the remembrance,
There is peace in the knowing
That he was hers,
And it was beautiful,

And that he was beautiful.
So that, like the sun in April showers,
Her smile breaks through the tears.
So much to smile for,
So much to be thankful for,
So much to live for
Still.

Unbroken

The crumbling,
The falling,
The drowning
Happens when you let your tests define you.
Heartbroken.
Abused.
Unemployed.
Single mum.
Difficult marriage.
Miscarried.
Divorced.
Widowed.
Alone.

Don't let your life's hurdles become
Your lens,
Don't let those struggles
Consume your identity.
You are more than those tests.
You always were.
Now all you have to do is believe it.

Walking Wounded

We are all walking, wounded,
Carrying our pain on the inside.
And though our faces are smiling,
Our hearts are frozen.
Thaw, little heart,
Yield.
It is done now.
Yours is to embrace the pain
And grow strong from it.

For this test
Was not sent to break you,
But to make you rise,
Like a phoenix from the ashes.
Ah, yes, you will rise,
By His Grace,
Scar tissue masked
By the smile on your face.

Small Kindnesses

The small kindnesses,
The tender mercies,
The moments of joy,
The flashes
of relief
Don't make up for the loss.
Not entirely.
But they help.
They help to remind you
That you have permission to smile,
To feel joy
And love
And gratitude,
In spite of the loss,
Or maybe because of it.

Because with every difficulty,
There is ease
If we open our arms
To embrace it.
His promise is true.

Take the Time

Take the time to rest
Dear One.
Breathe in
And out.
Take the time to mend
Your broken wing.
Take the time to choose
Which song to sing.
Take the time to heal
From pain unspoken.
Take the time to consider
The path you've chosen.
By His Grace
You will soar once more,
Higher and freer

Than you ever did before,
When the fire blazes again
From your very core,
'Til you finally meet your Beloved
On that distant shore.
For now
Just breathe.
In
And out.

Strange

Isn't it strange
That we love
Although the promise of loss
Is ever present?
Isn't it strange
That we hold
Although the threat of separation
Is always there?
Isn't it aastrange
That we birth
Although the inevitability of death
Is a constant
Constant
Reminder?
Isn't it strange?

Isn't it strange
That our hearts can break
And heal
And break,
Only to heal again?
Scar tissue
Crisscrossing
Like embroidery,
Holding it together,
Just like we hold it together,
Just like He holds us together.
Aren't we strange?
Aren't we strange...
And wonderful?

Love Now

Wouldn't you like
To be able to say
That you didn't waste a moment?
Didn't waste a moment on petty squabbles,
Or holding grudges,
Or those tiny daily cruelties that become so commonplace.
Too commonplace.

Wouldn't you like
To be able to say
That you woke up each morning
And kissed his eyelids
And thanked him
And told him how your heart melts when he holds your child,

That you long for his touch
Even though you've had a hard day?
Just a touch
Because you've had a hard day
And because his touch is all you need.

Wouldn't you like
To be able to say
That you made du'a for her every night
That her name fell off your tongue when in sujood
Just like the words 'You're gorgeous',
'I love you'
And 'I'm sorry' rolled off your tongue?
Easily.
Freely.
No price to pay.

Because no price is too high
To pay for her smile,
To see her relax
And know that she is loved.

Wouldn't you like
To be able to say
That you didn't miss a chance
To look them in the eyes
And listen to the long drawn-out story of their day?
To still all other thoughts,
To put everything else on hold,
To truly be there in the moment.
To open your heart to them,
To tell them about your childhood,
To share your dreams and plans with them.
To always end the night with a prayer,
A story and a kiss.

Wouldn't you like to say
That those you loved
Knew they were loved
Each and every day?

One day might be a day too late.
One night might be a night too long.
Don't wait.
Love like you mean it.
Love deep.
Love strong.
Love now.

JazakAllahu khairan for joining me on this journey.
Don't let a moment pass you by.
Na'ima B.

With special thanks to my EM sisters. I couldn't have done it without you, girls.

xxx

Other publications by Sisters Awakening Press

'Catch Me' is a collection of prose and poetry for those who want to reflect and seekers of pause and introspection. Through her weave of words, award-winning writer Na'ima B. Robert takes readers on a journey where admonitions are potent, wounds are laid bare then swathed, and the soul is soothed with hope of revival and renewal.

For reviews, previews and submissions, visit www.sistersawakening.com

Lightning Source UK Ltd.
Milton Keynes UK
UKHW022219111119
353319UK00005B/136/P